An Enneagram Murder Mystery

DRESSED
TO THE
NINES

TRACY HIGLEY

STONEWATER
BOOKS

~ *Welcome* ~

You're about to step into a story that functions on two levels, as both a murder mystery and an exploration of the Enneagram. As you seek to identify yourself with the characters in the story, as much as possible, try not to be influenced by the gender or profession of each character. Anyone can be any of the Enneagram numbers, and your type can manifest itself in many different professions or interests.

More information about each Enneagram type can be found at the end of the story, but don't skip to the end! Enjoy the story first!

ACT I

~ In which a Party
Leads to Murder ~

~ *Hugo* ~

Hugo muttered to himself as he turned onto the tree-lined road that led the way to Ashley's and Desmond's estate. In the deepening twilight, his headlights illuminated the intensifying snowfall, the crystalline fractals battling for supremacy over his wiper blades.

Ashley's 40th birthday notwithstanding, this party should have been cancelled due to bad weather.

He squinted into the blizzard, ratcheted up the *screetch* of his wipers, and gripped the wheel. Someone at this awful party was sure to rhapsodize about "no two snowflakes being alike." He would smile and try not to mention that all those flakes could easily be categorized into eight broad classifications, with about eighty variants. For some reason, no one ever seemed to appreciate that bit of information.

Why had he even been invited to this party? Yes, he'd worked for Ashley and United Chemical for seven years, but they weren't exactly *friends*. Friendly colleagues, perhaps. She respected his work, appreciated the contribution his research was making, to the corporate ledger as well as to the world. And Ashley was a hard-working, driven woman whom he admired.

Especially since she mostly left him alone in his lab to conduct his research in peace. But partying together? Not so much.

It must have been Desmond's idea to invite him. Ashley's husband sometimes reminded him of a golden retriever. A big, blond, friendly golden retriever. Hugo found the man a bit exhausting, truth to be told. Though to be fair, Hugo found many people exhausting. His feelings of social awkwardness made events like this one draining.

Something ran across the road — a deer? — and Hugo braked, sending the car into a fishtail. He righted his angle and tried to relax tense muscles. He'd left a good book at home to come out into this weather, to a party that was certain to be uncomfortable. It wasn't that he disliked people. The opposite, really. He found most of them fascinating in their own right. But he was useless with small talk. He usually kept to the fringe of most social gatherings, observing. Until inevitably, some well-meaning and fun-loving sort would pity him and drag him into an inane conversation, little-knowing they had increased his discomfort, rather than assuaged it.

Like Felicia.

Hugo cringed and closed his eyes for an instant against the swirling whiteness. Every time he encountered Ashley's younger sister the woman seemed intent on "drawing him out of his shell."

If he had a shell, Felicia's efforts felt more like cracking it open than drawing him out.

Felicia would surely be here for Ashley's birthday tonight, rapping her party-stick against him.

He took a deep breath of the chilled air and steeled himself for what was to come. A few hours, that's all it was. He would do what needed to be done. Then stand around, chat with the other party-goers, smile and raise a glass to Ashley, and be on his way, back to his book. Back to the comfortable space inside his head with his own thoughts and ideas.

Although at the rate this snow was closing in on him, his car might be buried in it by the time the party ended, and they'd all be stranded.

And that would not be a good thing.

~ *Vera* ~

Vera glanced into her rearview mirror at the headlights approaching where she'd pulled off the road, at the end of Ashley's and Desmond's long driveway.

Concerned about the forecasted snow, Vera vacated her house with twenty minutes to spare, just in case she ran into trouble. But then she'd feared seeming over-eager if she arrived on their doorstep so early, so she'd pulled off the road, into the suffocating silence, to wait. Now, she slipped the invitation out of her purse and checked the start time once more, just to be sure. Yes, 6:00. And the headlights rushing at her were probably those of another guest.

She swung into the drive, rolled the open gate, and peered toward the distant house. The windows glowed like beady yellow eyes. The long drive had disappeared under a white shroud, but thankfully she'd visited enough to steer a straight course to the circular loop in front of the estate. She kept her hands tight on the wheel and aimed for those yellow eyes. The lights in her rearview felt too close, like a stalker.

It had been kind of Desmond to invite her to the party. But of course, Desmond was always kind. Even if Ashley was working too hard to notice. She shook her head at the thought that seemed unfair to Ashley. Too many of those thoughts lately. Ashley was the best boss she'd ever had. Vera's only goal right now was to keep Ashley from doing something stupid. The few emails she'd seen in the past couple of weeks had her worried. Yes, she was prone to worry, but in this situation it was warranted. Ashley didn't always know what was best for her, and it was part of Vera's job to watch out for potential dangers, wasn't it? Being an executive assistant wasn't all about pencil-sharpening and getting coffee. Ashley paid her to be cautious. Or maybe Vera was being too cautious? Was she? Maybe tonight would hold the answers.

She sighed at her typical second-guessing and tried to set aside her anxiety to focus on the party.

She'd try to have fun, despite the guilt she was attempting to ignore. Wouldn't it be fun to spend the evening with some coworkers and Ashley's closest friends? It was so nice that she'd been included. She never felt completely confident in how Ashley viewed her, so the party invitation should feel like a warm hug. Even if it was a hug from Desmond.

The slippery drive to the house terminated in front of a stone fountain, and she exhaled in relief. She hadn't wrecked her car. She parked in the circular drive, as close to the front steps as she could. Ashley's huge, English-style country mansion had wide stone steps flanked by potted trees and scary-looking gargoyles, a decorating choice that always bothered her. As though people wanted to frighten their guests from their entrance.

Vera glanced over her shoulder to the backseat. The overnight bag she'd packed, ready for the potential of getting snowed in, lay there. Best to leave it in the car until she was actually invited, right? Instead, she grabbed the small, gold-wrapped box on the front seat, slipped it into her purse, emerged from her car into the sharp, cold air, and locked it behind her.

She blinked against the headlight glare that followed her into the estate and parked behind her. A moment later Hugo emerged and she gave a small wave. He was a nice guy, a little older than she, but also single. Around the office they jokingly called him "Professor." She was fairly sure he liked it. A sudden pang of anxiety — was Desmond trying to set the two of them up?

"Ready for a fun evening?" she called into the snow.

"Sure."

Hugo's answer seemed less than convincing, but she didn't press it.

He approached and held out an arm, as though expecting her to link hers with it, and nodded toward the front door above them. "Those steps look treacherous." He looked at her feet with a slight twitch of a smile. "And so do those shoes."

Grateful for the steady arm, she leaned on him as they ascended the steps.

A nice guy, yes. But she hoped he wasn't getting any ideas. Because that would just be awkward.

~ *Desmond* ~

Desmond studied the table setting in the wood-paneled dining room one final time. Headlights circled the drive outside and swept a harsh glare across the candlelit room. He'd taken care to ensure that everything was perfect for Ashley's party.

It had to be. Especially tonight.

Satisfied with the sparkling silver and china, the crystal centerpiece overflowing with white tulips — Ashley's favorite — and the crisp linen napkins expertly folded into tiny swans, Desmond headed for the Great Room to check if the fire needed wood before the first guests arrived.

On the far side of the massive room, the fire roared in the center of a high stone wall, casting a flickering glow against the wood-beamed cathedral ceiling. The room was comfortably warm against the chill of the storm, but not too warm, with the scent of woodsmoke hanging in the air.

His guests would enjoy themselves tonight, he'd make sure of it. He'd arranged everything they could want for an enjoyable evening. There were enough alcoves in the giant room for Hugo to hide, probably with a book selected from one of the floor-to-ceiling bookshelves. Enough seating areas for his brother

Rowan to lounge across. Vera would hover near Ashley, no doubt, while Ashley's sister Felicia would never stop moving. Ashley's best friend Lily was easy to please, thank goodness. He'd invited the other two, Charity and Grant, even though he barely knew them, since Ashley wouldn't consider the party complete without some networking opportunities.

The doorbell gonged, heavy and ominous, and Desmond pulled himself from the obsessive thoughts over everyone's enjoyment. Maybe one of these days he'd think about what *he* might enjoy at a party. But today was not that day. He just needed to get through this night.

He glanced toward the foyer, but there was no sign of Ashley on the stairs. She would still be upstairs, perfecting her outfit until she could make a grand entrance looking terrific.

Hugo and Vera stood outside the door, shoulders hunched against the snow.

"Did you two come together?"

Vera's eyes widened and she glanced sideways at Hugo. "What? No!" She laughed, a nervous little sound, and shook her head. "We just arrived at the same time. Hugo was kind enough to keep me from breaking my neck on the steps."

Desmond peered past her. "Do those steps need

clearing off again already? I put some salt down—"

"May we come in?" Hugo shouldered past him a bit.

"Of course - I'm so sorry!" Desmond pulled away from the door, torn between wanting to welcome his first two guests and wanting to clear off those steps for the guests who had not yet arrived. "Please, let me take your coats."

He brushed the snow off Vera's raincoat and Hugo's wool pea coat, hung both on the antlered coat tree in the foyer, and extended an arm toward the Great Room. "Come in, get warm."

When the two had seated themselves, somewhat awkwardly across the room from each other, Desmond eyed the front door. "I'm just going to sweep off those front steps. Be right back."

He jogged out to get the snow cleared, cursing himself for not offering either Vera or Hugo a drink first. But he couldn't be everywhere at once, could he? Maybe it would occur to Ashley to come down and play hostess. But he knew his wife, so maybe not.

Then again, did he really know her? Or was he losing her? Desmond's gut twisted in apprehension. One way or another, he'd get his answer tonight.

~ *Ashley* ~

Ashley held one of the diamond drop earrings Desmond had given her on her last birthday against her right ear and turned her head to survey the effect in the gilt-edged mirror. Did the earrings say "success" or did they say "show-off"? She huffed in impatience, then made the decision. She'd wasted enough time already getting ready. The right dress, the right shoes. Hair perfect, jewelry perfect. It was exhausting keeping up with the reputation she'd carefully established. Just once, she'd like to come down to a dinner party in flannel sweatpants. Too bad she didn't own any.

She multi-tasked through jabbing the earrings through her earlobes, slipping on shoes, and checking her hair one last time, and nearly tripped over the area rug in the center of her dressing room.

She should have left work earlier, given herself more time to get ready. But there was never enough time in the day to get her work done, so cutting the day short didn't seem like a workable option. No matter how often Desmond asked her to do it.

The thought of Desmond brought the inevitable stab of guilt. She shoved it down. No time for that, either.

"Ashley?" A familiar female voice drifted in from

the far side of her bedroom.

"In here," she called.

Lily was in the doorway a moment later. "Well, you look great, as always."

Lily had been her best friend since college, and wouldn't have said a negative thing if Ashley truly had been decked out in flannel sweatpants.

Ashley crossed the dressing room and hugged her friend.

"Happy Birthday, girl."

Lily's hugs always provoked an instant sense of stillness, like she'd just been dropped onto the grassy bank beside a mountain lake. She'd always needed that calm in her chaotic life. Ashley held on for an extra moment.

"Hey, are you alright?" Lily held her at arm's length. "What's going on? You nervous about tonight? It's just family and friends. And people from work. And that CEO guy. And what's-her-name with the non-profit." She grinned, then grew serious when Ashley didn't laugh. "You're not worried —"

Ashley shook her head. "I'm fine." There wasn't time to discuss the gnawing guilt. "Let's go downstairs."

Lily held out a hand and bowed into a curtsy. "Would you like your lady-in-waiting to precede you down the stairs, or follow in your train?"

Ashley slapped Lily's hand away, laughing. "Shut

up."

Despite her light tone, Ashley felt a sharp tension between her shoulders. This party had to go well, and there were so many ways it could go wrong.

The two descended the steps together, though as they turned into the Great Room, Lily held back to let Ashley enter first.

All eyes turned toward her. She hoped she was pulling off the "I've got my act together" look.

Desmond leaned against the stone wall beside the fire, and her head researcher Hugo, sitting on the leather sofa, jumped to his feet.

She lifted her chin, smiled, and held out her hands. "Apologies, friends, for my late entrance. And welcome."

Her executive assistant Vera stepped beside her, eying Lily behind her somewhat nervously. "Happy birthday, Ashley." She leaned in for a quick kiss on the cheek.

"Thank you, Vera."

Hugo dipped his head, offered a happy birthday that sounded a bit more like a condolence, and sat back down.

"Well, here she is, the birthday girl at last! Now the party can begin!"

Ashley turned to the voice from a dark corner of the

Great Room. Her sister Felicia strolled out of the shadows.

"Ah, Felicia, everyone knows the party only begins when *you* arrive."

Felicia leaned one shoulder forward coyly and fluttered her eyelashes. "You flatter me, sister."

Desmond was at her side a moment later, handing her a glass of something bubbly, as though he were the butler. She took the drink, not meeting his eyes.

The doorbell rang, Desmond went to answer, and Charity entered the room, followed by Grant.

Desmond had not been happy when she suggested these two be invited. They weren't family or close friends, not even close colleagues. Charity headed up a non-profit, as though eager to prove herself worthy of her name, and Ashley had recently been polishing the image of United Chemical by helping with the woman's pet project.

Behind her came Grant, CEO of Corr Industries, a company she'd been in talks with regarding a possible merger or acquisition. The man exuded charisma and power — she could feel it from across the room.

Yes, it was her birthday. But that was no reason to waste a perfectly good opportunity for improving the company's bottom line. Social events like this often led to important business deals. Desmond and Lily would both say she was a workaholic. She couldn't seem to relax, even after a win, always on to the next challenge. But it was people like Ashley who got things done in the world, and she wouldn't have it any other way.

The front door opened on its own and the wind kicked in a few snowflakes behind the last guest to arrive. Desmond's starving-artist brother Rowan paused in the open door, as though conscious of the dramatic effect of the snowy night behind his silhouette. His eyes went right to Ashley, and as always she felt like he was reading her secrets.

She looked away. Tonight, especially, she wanted to keep her secrets to herself.

~ *Rowan* ~

Rowan stood in the doorway for a long moment, taking in the cozy scene inside the gorgeous house, the tight little group by the blazing fire, drinks in hand, looking like something from a Great Gatsby remake. He didn't even know all of them, but it was clear they belonged there together. Elegant and carefree. He was glad he'd arrived late, since it made for less time feeling like an outsider.

Desmond crossed the room, shut the door, and pulled Rowan's coat from his shoulders. "Glad you're here, brother."

He forced a smile for Desmond, who deserved better from him. His brother was always there for him, even willing to bail him out with a few bucks when things got too tight.

Although, let's face it, the money was really Ashley's. This house wasn't bought on a high school guidance counselor's paycheck.

Even so, one of these days he'd stop needing to rely on his brother's handouts. It wouldn't be so bad if Desmond really believed in Rowan's art. But Desmond didn't know real art from department store wall-trash, and his brother was more about rescuing the underachieving artist than being his patron.

"Rowan," Ashley crossed the room, hands held out to him in welcome.

He clasped them and leaned in for a kiss. "Happy birthday, sis-in-law."

"You are sweet. I'm so glad you're here."

Her words were kind, but it was sometimes hard to tell how Ashley was really feeling.

"The house looks amazing." He took in the orange glow of the lamps, the heavy drapes, and nodded toward the fire. "Like a beacon of warmth as I emerged from the pitiless storm."

Ashley turned to the group in the Great Room. "My brother-in-law, everyone. Our artist and poet."

Introductions ensued, and Rowan nodded politely as Desmond gave a brief synopsis on the charitable Charity, and Grant who was some sort of titan of industry. He'd met Ashley's friend Lily and assistant Vera on other occasions, as well as Professor Hugo. And of course Ashley's sister Felicia was unforgettable.

Rowan had entered the house feeling hopeful that the party would be subdued rather than jocular. He did better with low-key. Overly cheerful people made him queasy. But there was something more than low-key happening here tonight. Some kind of quiet undercurrent of tension. Rowan was usually more sensitive to these things than most people, so perhaps it was just his imagination.

And what else was he feeling? Perhaps a bit of envy. They all seemed so successful.

He drifted around the edges of the various conversations happening in the room and watched each face in turn. Vera's eyes darted between each guest, as though performing a constant threat assessment, but from what he'd seen of her in previous situations, that was her norm. Lily seemed at ease, as always, though she did have a watchful eye on Ashley as though she also sensed something wrong.

Felicia was a live wire of energy, bouncing between conversations the way she'd jumped between occupations in the years Rowan had known her. But was there a bit of anxiety, under her high spirits? A feverish sort of brightness in her eyes?

And then his glance circled to Hugo, and his heart jumped. The man was staring at Rowan from his position on the opposite edge of the group, as though they shared the common pursuit of observation.

Although while Rowan was painting each guest's emotions on the canvas of his mind's eye, he suspected Hugo was classifying and filing each into a mental spreadsheet. Instead of bonding him to the other man, the shared observation only left Rowan feeling more isolated.

He sighed, feeling the room's energy, tension, and

anxiety in a wave that receded and left him a little depressed. Would his latest failure be discussed before he was able to do what he must?

It was going to be a long night.

~ *Grant* ~

Grant wondered for the hundredth time what the heck he was doing at this party.

If it weren't for how much he needed this deal with United Chemical, he would never have agreed to attend a party where he was not either the host or the guest of honor. It wasn't an ego thing. He just felt more comfortable when he was in charge. It had been excruciating to enter a room where he knew no one but Ashley.

Though it was quite a room. From the marble bust of somebody-apparently-important in the front hall, to the mounted elk over the mantel, it was like he'd stepped into Victorian England.

He eyed that elk. Was it real? Desmond didn't seem the kill-and-stuff type. Maybe Ashley fired the kill shot. He stifled a laugh.

He checked out the group once more, trying to get his bearings. There were two interesting sets of siblings. The two brothers — Desmond and Rowan — nothing like each other. And then the two sisters — Ashley and Felicia — even less alike. He mentally rehearsed the rest of the names in the room.

So, stuck here for the night, knowing almost no one, trying to keep the truth from coming out and having very little control. Not his idea of fun.

Although he'd managed to take charge of the little conversation he was having with Charity and Lily, even throwing out a bit of bait to Charity about a better strategy for the mission she was on, to clean up the city. He always did like a bit of a verbal skirmish before dinner.

He held up a hand to stop Charity's self-righteous tirade. "Look, I admire your passion, Charity. And I totally agree that giving kids a clean and safe place to play is important. I'm just saying that if you don't stop the problem at the source, you'll get one block cleaned up, and as soon as you move on to the next, all your work in that last place will go *poof*." He flicked his fingers outward on that last word, and the woman's face darkened ominously. Oh, he'd picked a good conversation partner.

Lily leaned in, as though to physically get between the two before a punch was thrown. "Grant, perhaps Ashley has told you how committed she is to Charity's project. She's donating quite a bit of the proprietary paint solvent that she and Hugo developed, to help Charity get rid of unsightly graffiti."

He raised his eyebrows. "To give the gangs another clean canvas to work on, you mean? I'm telling you I'm sure there's a better way to get the results you're after."

Charity rolled her eyes. "If you have such great ideas, why aren't you signing up to help, instead of taking shots?"

Lily's laugh was like cool water being sprinkled on smoking embers. "Grant, certainly your company is involved in some charitable endeavors as well?"

He held up his hands in surrender. "Just trying to keep the conversation honest. But I get it. We're here for a party. And really, Charity, I do admire the work you do. Don't mind my bluntness. It's my worst quality."

Or so he'd been told. In truth, he rather liked that quality in himself. Honesty was underrated, and most people he met were far too eager to please. Better to get the truth out there and deal with it. That's when you could really do some good in the world.

But as the thought ran through him, he looked away, glancing at Ashley and feeling the guilt. There were things she didn't know. About Corr Industries. About him. His life had gotten out of control, and he didn't like it one bit.

But tonight. Tonight all that was going to change.

~ *Lily* ~

It was a relief to Lily when Desmond began to move the group toward the dining room and the scent of roasted meat. The conversation with Grant and Charity had gotten tense, and her efforts to lessen the tension had been unsuccessful. She'd always had the gift of being able to see both sides of an argument and bring people together in the middle, but those were two high-energy and forceful people. How had she gotten in the middle of *that* conversation?

She also regretted not sticking closer to Ashley. These past couple of weeks had her concerned, but she hadn't confronted her friend. Better to be there as someone to lean on than create a conflict by making waves. Although later… she planned to do something very unlike her.

"Lily, the flowers are amazing." Ashley ran her fingers over the edge of a white tulip, then spoke to the group still finding their name cards at the table. "Those of you who don't know, Lily is a florist."

Grant chuckled. "Guess that was inevitable, eh?"

Lily smiled sweetly, though the comment she'd heard a thousand times always bothered her a bit.

"Yes, I suppose it was my destiny."

Destiny, or passivity? That was the question that always reared its head when someone made the "inevitable" comment. People seemed to think she'd floated into the floral industry on the current of her first name, as though she hadn't any will of her own, any better opinion of what she should do with her life. But she wasn't unhappy. It was a stress-free life, just as she preferred. Why should she fight when something felt simple and right?

Perhaps that was why everyone seemed surprised by her friendship with Ashley. Ever since their college days, her best friend had been one hundred percent drive and ambition and energy. Twenty years ago that had looked different — more like a frantic climb to the top of every campus club, of their sorority, even every relationship.

Which was why the past couple of weeks had Lily worried. She'd seen glimpses of that old Ashley, the one who had been reckless with her affections. And she didn't like it.

Desmond had taken care to seat people carefully around the table, it seemed. Ashley was at the head, with four people down each side. Thankfully, Grant and Charity had the table between them, with Charity on Ashley's left, probably because Desmond realized the woman knew no one else at the party. He'd seated himself on Ashley's right and Grant next to himself for the same reason, no doubt. Next to Charity, Hugo slid into his chair. Had the man said anything since arriving? Felicia was next to Hugo. Lily smiled to herself at the man's clear discomfort. Her own spot was on the other side of Felicia. She liked Ashley's sister, though the woman loved turbulence the way Lily loved tranquility.

On the other side, after Desmond and Grant, sat Rowan and Vera.

Yes, he'd done a good job, alternating the familiar with unfamiliar, the talkers with the quiet ones. She smiled over at him, hoping to signal her approval.

But Desmond's eyes were on Ashley, and the look on his face brought her fear of impending conflict surging back.

Clearly, Desmond was not happy.

~ *Charity* ~

Charity had never seen a table set so gloriously. Everything worked together to create a sparkling, flawless elegance. Even the flatware was in perfect, perpendicular alignment. The beauty of it settled her nerves a bit, after the challenging conversation with Grant.

The man was blunt, as he had admitted, and Charity had been a bit put off by his argumentativeness, considering they had just met. But another part of her was impressed. He had a forcefulness about him, a passion about his ideas, that matched her own.

Even though Charity probably got as many comments as Lily did about following in the footsteps of her name, she knew herself to be only one small step from having her humanitarian passion turn to anger. There was just so much wrong with the world, and at times it all enraged her. She knew she'd run out of time before she could put it all right, and that only made her more furious.

It was a flaw she was always trying to eradicate, this tendency to jump to anger when things did not go as she knew they ought. Or when people didn't do the right thing. Yes, there it was, that jolt of anger at the recent disappointment. It wasn't Ashley's fault, and

Charity didn't blame her. But she was still angry.

She tried to shake off the conversation with Grant and her displeasure over the week's events, and simply enjoy the beautiful perfection of the dinner party. Ashley's contributions to CleanCity had been generous, and she'd appreciated the woman's savvy business sense, but to be invited to her birthday party was an unexpected pleasure.

A beautiful salad with a tangy vinaigrette seemed to appear like magic, though of course it was Desmond who served. She offered to bring food from the kitchen, but he seemed uncomfortable to be on the receiving side of help.

The meal proceeded like clockwork, with each course more delicious than the last. The conversations ebbed and flowed. At one point Desmond came back with drink in hand. Ashley eyed the drink and then Desmond, but said nothing.

Charity had one fascinating little discussion with Hugo, about his work on the paint solvent, but when it dwindled, he excused himself from the room, probably to check his phone, which he seemed unable to put away for the extent of the meal.

Ashley was talking to Desmond and Grant, leaving Charity free to assess the other guests. Ashley's assistant — Vera, wasn't it? — seemed restless. She left the room during both the soup and the main course, which seemed a bit rude. Rowan seemed a bit... sad. All around, it felt like everyone was waiting for something to happen.

Halfway through the chocolate turtle cheesecake and aromatic coffee, Vera got up and peered through the window. Grant had been holding forth on some topic, with the attention of most of the table on him. That attention did not include Hugo next to her. He had his phone out again, surreptitiously looking at it half-hidden under the table.

"It's like a solid wall of white out there," Vera said. She turned back to the table, chewing her lip. "I hope we're able to get out to the road."

"Doesn't matter." Hugo pulled his phone out and placed it on the table. "I just checked the local situation. The highway has been shut down." He turned his phone screen-down and lifted his head. "None of us is going anywhere tonight."

Hugo looked as though he'd just announced a death, his face so depressed that Charity nearly laughed. Perhaps being stuck at a dinner party was a fate worse than death for him.

Desmond lifted his glass. "This house was built for a crowd, and there are only two of us."

Beside her, Charity felt Ashley physically tense.

"So," Desmond was saying, "plenty of guest rooms.

You are all welcome to make a night of it."

She glanced down the table, taking in each expression. Clearly, being snowed in represented an adventure to some and a nightmare to others. On her part, she wasn't thrilled with the disruption to her routine, but she also felt that driving unsafely should be avoided, and was glad that Desmond had offered to put them up.

Why then, did she get the sense that something terrible was about to happen?

~ *Felicia* ~

Felicia elbowed Hugh in the ribs as soon as he'd finished his gloomy pronouncement. "So this'll be fun, huh?" She grinned at his obvious displeasure.

There was something about this guy that always made her want to goad him. She actually liked him immensely, though he no doubt thought she tortured him for pleasure. It wasn't sadistic, though. She actually saw something in him that, oddly, reminded her of herself. There was a deep fascination with life there, one she also felt. An exhilaration that came with the rush of ideas. Granted, her fascination hadn't taken her into books and research and all-around-genius stuff. She'd been more about trying out every interesting experience she could, trying to find the thing that felt just right. But still, they had something in common even if Hugo didn't see it.

She'd been looking forward to tonight's party ever since Desmond invited her, determined to make it a party they'd all remember. And now it would be extended, which was perfect. She'd get them to move back to the Great Room soon, and break out some games, maybe. Get everyone busy, having fun. She had some ideas of her own. But could she find a way to lighten the heavy atmosphere?

In the meantime, she'd make the most of the table-talk. She'd already engaged Hugo enough to get on his nerves, and on her left, Lily was happy just being quiet.

Across from her, Rowan slouched in his chair, picking at his cheesecake.

"Lactose intolerant, Rowan?"

He lifted his heavy, indifferent lids to meet her gaze and half-smiled. He wasn't taking the bait. "Just watching my figure."

She grinned. She and Rowan were sort of the black sheep of their respective families. Felicia, with her über-successful sister Ashley, and Rowan, with comparisons to the saint-like Desmond. Black sheep had to stick together. She hoped Rowan would still like her after tonight.

"So, Felicia," Grant pulled her attention toward himself, "Desmond tells me you've had quite the interesting life."

She scowled good-naturedly at her brother-in-law, who sometimes talked too much, and took a sip of her dark roast before answering. "I suppose you could say that."

"Oh, don't be shy, Felicia." Ashley laughed. "You've had enough fun for five lifetimes already."

The comment was equal parts judgment and jealousy. A familiar mix whenever Ashley commented on her life.

"Tell them about the island."

She shrugged. "I worked for a couple of years on a private island, managing some rich guy's estate."

Grant seemed amused. "Sounds like the ultimate life for a party girl."

"Yeah, it was good therapy after scraping dead bodies off the street."

"Felicia!" Ashley sighed. "I apologize for my sister's lack of tact. Her years running ambulance as an EMT left her a little... indelicate."

"Sorry." Felicia frowned. "Seriously, it was good to decompress for awhile, but the place was too remote to live there forever."

Desmond joined in. "So she came back and started a catering business that did really well, but then got bored with it, so she decided to tend bar while she got her scuba-diving instructor license. Or was it ballerina first, and then scuba-diving?"

"Ha-ha." She made a face at Desmond, but it was good to see a bit of the old Desmond there. She'd been a little concerned that something was terribly wrong between her sister and brother-in-law.

"I'll have you all know, I haven't been a ballerina since grade school." She surveyed the table, and all of them seemed to be finished with their dessert. "So let's take this party out to the Great Room," she said. "We've got a storm outside, a warm fire inside, and good friends to share the evening with. What could be better?"

But the words were spoken with a humor she did not feel. Not with this crowd. Not tonight.

ACT II

~ In Which a Body
is Discovered ~

The group of nine adjourned to the low lighting of the Great Room, drifting away from the table in tense little clusters, some sooner than others.

Vera, Ashley, and Charity sank into the cozy seating area near the fireplace, with only enough room for the three of them, though it appeared that Vera was the extra, as Ashley and Charity continued an intense conversation begun in the dining room.

Hugo began perusing the bookshelves, while Desmond and Grant leaned on the bar at the side of the room, chatting.

Rowan appeared some minutes later and sank into an upholstered settee near the back of the room, closest to the front door.

Lily and Felicia were absent, though it was only a few minutes later that Lily drifted in, another piece of cheesecake on her plate. She glanced around the room, then sat in a chair by the window, eating her cheesecake and watching the snow.

Felicia whirled into the room some time later, waving something in her hand.

"Found them!" She held a deck of cards aloft.

Ashley frowned. "Why didn't you ask? We have several decks here, in the game closet." She pointed to a cabinet set into the wall in the corner.

Felicia shrugged. "I knew I'd seen some in a kitchen drawer somewhere once. Who's up for a game?"

No one responded.

"A little too tame, perhaps? I know what we need - Ashley, where's that poker table-top thing you bought last year? Still in the garage?"

Ashley glanced at her guests, as if trying to gauge whether anyone wanted to join in Felicia's forced fun. "Yes, I think so. Hanging on the back wall."

"Great." Felicia nodded toward Vera, still clearly on the outside of the conversation between Ashley and Charity. "Vera, would you go grab it, while I set up the table in here?"

"Sure." Vera seemed grateful for an escape.

The rest returned to their pursuits, while Felicia pulled a heavy mahogany table away from a window and started pulling chairs toward it.

A minute later, a horrible scream pierced the night air.

Each of them froze, eyes wide. Then glances met, surprise on each face.

Desmond moved first, toward the scream that seemed to come from the back of the house.

Ashley jumped up, as if she would stop him, but stood in place.

Grant followed close on Desmond's heels, leaving the rest gaping at each other.

A breath later, they all hurried toward the back hall, as if no one wanted to be left alone in the Great Room.

They arrived within seconds of each other, outside the kitchen door in the snow.

Vera stood over a dark bundle in the snow at her feet, trembling. Clearly, it was she who had uttered the terrible scream.

"It's — it's a — body!" She glanced down and then away quickly, as if she couldn't stand the sight. "He's dead — I'm sure of it!"

Felicia pushed through to the front of the little crowd and kneeled at the prostrate form. The rest of them took a step back to give her space, each no doubt remembering her ambulance training.

The body was lying on his side, facing away from the house, and appeared to be a man in a bulky winter coat. Beside him in the snow lay the poker table-top Vera had fetched from the garage.

Felicia felt for a pulse in the wrist and neck, pulled the coat open, leaned in closer to examine the face, then sat back on her heels.

"Vera is right. He's dead."

All eyes were on Felicia, as though she would somehow produce an explanation.

"What happened to him?" Grant asked.

Ashley's question overlapped Grant's. "Who is he?"

Felicia answered Grant, though spoke to the group. "I didn't see any obvious trauma. If I had to guess, I'd say he ingested some sort of poison. He has flecks of foam on his mouth, there's a strange smell, and his lips are oddly blue."

She turned back to the body, as if to verify her own statement, then started feeling in his pockets for some kind of identification. She stopped before pulling anything out, and leaned closer to the man's face. "Ashley... isn't this..." She glanced at Desmond, then back to Ashley. "Isn't this Vincent, your old college boyfriend?"

"What?" Ashley leaned back, her hand on her chest. Then took a step forward and leaned over the body.

Felicia turned him slightly, causing the rest of them to move back as though death were contagious.

Ashley gasped. "I — I haven't —" She looked back at Desmond. "Yes, yes, that's Vincent."

Desmond's face was as pale as the snow still falling.

Lily and Rowan both stepped toward the body at once. They'd all known Vincent back in their college days. In fact, it was through Vincent that Rowan and Ashley had met, and then Rowan introduced Ashley to his brother Desmond.

Charity glanced at Ashley. "Vincent? Not the Vincent that..."

Ashley nodded, her fingers over her mouth.

Silence descended, the eerie, unnatural silence of a heavy snowfall.

And then Charity was speaking at the back of the crowd. "Yes, we need police sent to this location. We've found a dead body in the snow."

The group turned at once to find Charity speaking into her phone, eyes fixed on the body. She spoke with the emergency operator for another moment, giving assurances that they had a trained professional on site who'd confirmed the death, then listening for a moment. "I understand. Thank you."

She gripped the phone with tight fingers. "The police can't get through because of the roads. They're not sure how long it will take. They've requested we cover the body, not touch anything, and leave the scene until they arrive."

Felicia nodded and pulled the man's coat partly over his face.

Ashley disappeared into the garage and returned with a blue plastic tarp held in her fingertips. She passed it to Felicia, who covered the body completely.

"That's all we can do," Felicia said. "Let's get inside before we freeze."

The group filed back into the house in silence.

Behind them, the poker table was already disappearing under the snow.

ACT III

~ In which an
Investigation Ensues ~

~ *Ashley* ~

Ashley was the first to arrive back in the Great Room, and it seemed disrespectful to the dead to simply reclaim her comfortable chair, so she paced in front of the fire.

The others ranged around the huge room, some standing, others sitting. All silent.

Desmond was quiet. Too quiet, she feared. She risked a glance at him. She couldn't read his face. Anger? Hurt? Or even worse, suspicion?

She turned away and saw that while she'd been watching Desmond, Hugo had been watching her. He stood with his back against the bar, arms folded over his chest.

Their eyes met, and he seemed to take her acknowledgment as an invitation to speak.

"So the dead man was your… college boyfriend?"

She nodded. "Yes. Yes, we dated. Before I met Desmond, of course."

"Of course."

Hugo's repetition of her words annoyed her. Did he suspect there was more?

Nevermind what Hugo thought. He worked for her. But none of this was going to look good for the company. She had just started to improve their image by working with Charity on the CleanCity project.

Even as she had the thought, she pushed it away. Why did she always feel like she had to make sure others saw her as accomplished and impressive? Always looking at herself through others' eyes, trying to be what they wanted or expected her to be?

Rowan made a derisive sound from where he sprawled across the couch. "Ash, you got the better deal when you ended up with Desmond, believe me."

"I haven't seen Vincent in more than ten years, though." She glanced again at her husband, guilt stirring in her chest.

"Really?" Grant's eyebrows lifted. "May I ask what an old college flame, whom you haven't seen in over ten years, was doing behind your house?"

She bristled. "How should I know?"

Lily touched her arm. "Had he been bothering you again?"

She pulled her arm away. Why did Lily have to bring up the past?

But Hugo had heard Lily's comment. "Bothering you? Again?"

She swallowed and surveyed the room. She hated to put her past mistakes on display for the entire crowd, but it seemed unavoidable. Especially since they were all looking at her like her hands were covered in blood. Or poison.

"He was — he wasn't a great guy back then, I guess."

Again a snort from Rowan.

"And I was less confident. Less sure of myself. I let him — mistreat me." She hated the way the confession sounded. Hated for anyone in this room to think of her as weak or even less-than-successful in her personal life.

Lily squeezed her shoulders. "But you ditched him eventually. That's what counts."

"So," Grant's response lingered in the air for a moment, unresolved. "He simply shows up dead behind your house after all these years?"

Ashley exhaled. How could she spin this to look less suspicious? To make herself look like less of a loser?

Rowan lifted his head. "Oh, please. Everyone knows that Ashley does everything perfectly. If she were going to murder someone, she wouldn't do it in her own backyard."

Ashley frowned. "Thanks, Rowan." The words emerged sounding a bit sarcastic, but she was actually cheered a bit at his back-handed compliment. At least it took the attention off her failure to stand up for herself back in college.

Felicia was nodding. "Agreed. Besides, Ashley works way too many hours in a day to have time for murder."

Her sister's attempt at humor fell flat.

"Then I ask again," Grant said, "Why was—"

"I invited him."

Ashley turned to Desmond, lips parted.

He was staring at the floor after this confession.

"What? Why?"

Desmond shrugged one shoulder. "I just… had a feeling. A feeling you two were seeing each other again. I wanted to see your reaction. When I brought him in as a surprise guest." He lifted his eyes to meet her open-mouthed expression. "I thought I would know. If I could watch your reaction."

"You thought—"

"Yes." Desmond's voice was overly loud now, a bit manic-sounding. "Yes, Ashley. I suspected that you and Vincent were having an affair."

~ *Desmond* ~

"That's insane!"

Desmond watched Ashley's eyes as she denied his accusation. When he had invited Vincent last week, he'd wanted to see her reaction when her ex-boyfriend showed up, but watching this reaction was almost as good.

Did he believe her?

And did she somehow find out about Vincent's invitation?

Grant crossed his arms. "I'm confused. It seems like most of you knew the victim?"

Desmond waited for Ashley to answer, but she'd gone silent, as though she'd checked out of the conversation.

He turned to Grant, nodding. "Ashley was a chemistry major in college, but she got involved with Vincent, who was an art major. It's how United Chemical got its start, really, when she became interested in the chemicals used in art restoration while she was — dating — Vincent." He nearly choked on the word "dating" for some reason. "My brother Rowan and Vincent were friends—"

"Not friends," Rowan piped up. "We knew each

other from art classes. The guy was a jerk."

Desmond took a breath. "My brother met Ashley when she was dating Vincent. When Ashley finally broke things off with him, Rowan introduced Ashley to me."

Grant turned to Ashley. "So, just trying to get this straight. Your sister Felicia and best friend Lily met Vincent back then as well?"

She nodded but said nothing.

Desmond watched her eyes again. Why was she not saying anything more? He'd set up this whole party, hoping to prove to himself that Ashley needed him. Loved him. Or maybe even to *get* her to love him more, if he was honest. He did often find himself taking care of everyone around him, and felt like he shouldn't ask others to take care of him. But now it had gone horribly wrong.

Felicia was still pacing the room, as though her energy was too intense to keep still. She'd added nothing to the conversation, but surely she remembered, as well as Rowan did, what a rotten person Vincent had been? Did Felicia think Desmond killed Vincent out of jealousy?

Charity, standing beside Desmond, injected herself into the conversation. "I think it's clear to everyone that Ashley was better off with Desmond, and that he loves her very much."

The statement drew attention to her, but didn't seem to have a point.

"Thanks, Charity."

Lily leaned in. "I think what Charity means to say is that Desmond is obviously a very warm and caring person."

"Not the type to murder someone in a jealous rage? Is that what you meant, Charity?"

Charity tried to smile. "I just don't think we should be accusing—"

"Actually, murders are committed by people in love every day," Grant said. "Being passionate about someone doesn't mean—"

"Grant, please!" Ashley seemed to wake up enough to stop the man's flow of words.

But did her objection seem a bit forced? Desmond couldn't tell.

"This is all crazy," Ashley still held everyone's attention. "Just because I dated someone in college, even if he was a bit of a jerk, doesn't mean I would murder him at my birthday party." She pointed at her sister. "Felicia had a crush on Vincent back then, too, but obviously no one would accuse her of murder, so why me?"

Felicia's head snapped up at the revelation, but she said nothing.

Desmond had forgotten about that. Felicia *had* been after Vincent first, hadn't she?

Grant made a sound in the back of his throat.

What was the man thinking?

"Did someone accuse you of murder, Ashley?" Grant asked. "It seemed to me the opposite statement was made."

"I don't know." She held up her hands. "I don't know. This is all insane. It's all some kind of misunderstanding, I'm sure."

"Little hard to misunderstand a dead body, sis."

No one responded to Felicia's good point.

Grant turned to Desmond. "May I ask you something?"

Desmond shrugged. "Whatever. Let's just clear the air."

"What made you think that your wife was having an affair with her ex-boyfriend from college?"

From out of the shadows, Vera's quiet voice answered the question.

"I'm afraid that would be my fault."

~ *Vera* ~

Vera had been hoping that she could stay out of all this conversation. It was the only way to avoid suspicion. It was too easy for people to turn on you, she knew from experience. It probably wouldn't take much for someone to paint her as a homicidal maniac.

But it had to come out. At least the part she'd played in Vincent being invited to this party. Hopefully no more than that.

Everyone was watching her from all their places around the room. She tried to breathe out the tension in her chest. The sound in the cavernous room still somehow felt muted, dead. Was it getting hotter?

"I was the one who told Desmond that Ashley was involved with Vincent again."

Grant frowned. "You knew him too?"

"No! I mean, I knew *of* him, I guess… just from Ashley's correspondence…"

Charity spoke up again. "I really don't think it's right that we are talking about any of this. It seems like a matter for the police—"

Vera bit her lip, hoping they all would agree.

"We have all night," Grant said. "Perhaps we can come to an answer before the police even arrive."

Charity sighed and shook her head, as though Grant were a disobedient child.

Desmond came to Vera's rescue, not surprisingly. "Vera told me that she'd seen quite a bit of email back and forth between Ashley and Vincent. To Ashley's private email address, so she didn't know the contents. Only Vincent's name and the subject lines."

Grant looked at her. "And that was enough for you to go to your employer's husband…"

Vera squashed down the thoughts she'd had for poor Desmond.

"I was curious," she felt herself blushing, "so I looked Vincent up online. Saw that he was a big art gallery dealer. And then I remembered Ashley mentioning him years ago."

"I see." Grant nodded once as though satisfied.

But when had that man let anything go? No, he would keep her in his sights, for sure. Her stomach fluttered.

"That doesn't seem like you, Vera," Felicia said. "Ashley always says that you're the most committed assistant she's ever had. That you'd fight like a mama bear to protect her. I'm surprised you'd betray her that way."

That stung. She *did* feel guilty over what she'd done. But because she was always trying to find the place where everything was secure, where she felt supported in her job and life and *everything*, she'd felt like he had to do something to remove the threat. Why couldn't she trust herself more?

Vera rubbed her palm. "If anyone would kill someone to protect Ashley, it would be Lily!"

She knew how outrageous the accusation sounded, but she had to get the attention to shift away from her. As expected, all eyes turned to Lily.

The florist held up her hands. "That's true, I'm afraid."

Vera nearly rolled her eyes. The woman was so inclined to agree with everyone that she'd even agree to her own motive for murder.

Ashley huffed. "Lily is the least likely person to commit murder that I've ever known."

"Exactly!" Vera spread her hands. "And it's *always* the least likely person!"

There were a few quiet chuckles around the room, but no one seemed eager to agree with her.

"So, Vera." Grant rapped his knuckles on the black granite bar top and brought the conversation back to her.

"Based on a few emails *that you did not read*," he stressed those words as though to crack a confession from her, "you told Desmond that you believed Ashley was having an affair?"

"No!" This was going terribly. "No, I just told him that Ashley was back in contact with Vincent. Did I do the wrong thing? I didn't even know if the emails were personal. Besides, sometimes Charity was cc'd on those emails, too, and from the subject lines it seemed like she was angry."

Desmond's jaw dropped. "What? You never told me that!"

Anxiety flooded her. What had she done?

~ *Charity* ~

Charity looked up at the mention of her name, from where she'd been leaning over Hugo's position in an overstuffed chair on the side of the room. The researcher had barely spoken through all of Grant's questions, but she noticed he had a pen and small notepad in front of him, where he seemed to be taking notes.

"You neglected to mention you knew the victim as well, Charity." Grant's question sounded like he was daring her to answer.

Charity tried to relax, to not sound defensive. "I didn't *know* him. Not really."

Grant waited, as did they all, but finally spoke. "You think we're going to let you leave it at that?"

She sighed. "Not that it's any of your business, but, fine. Ashley connected me with Vincent a few months ago. She thought he would be interested in my CleanCity project, especially the graffiti removal and subsequent art to be painted in the cleaned areas." At this, she glared at Grant, who hadn't listened long enough to hear the entire plan before he insisted the areas would be covered in graffiti again. "Apparently, Vincent has done very well as an art dealer over the years. He promised a very large donation to my organization."

"And yet, Vera tells us your emails were angry."

"Because he gave me the shaft."

The accusation sounded too enraged. She should have toned it down. She did feel guilty over all of it. In fact, she always felt guilty. People sometimes accused her of being too critical. But she was as hard on herself as she was on anyone else. She had high standards, that's all, and believed in doing things right. That's why this whole situation was so… upsetting.

She returned her attention to Grant and tried to soften her tone.

"Apparently, Vincent decided to go in a different direction with his charitable contributions this year."

"I see. And how did that make you feel?"

"What are you, my therapist?"

Hugo tapped his pen on his notepad. "Perhaps there should be no accusations until we have all the facts."

Grant stared him down. "I don't work for you."

Rowan laughed. "This is so much better than playing cards."

Charity still needed to defend herself. "It made me angry, I will admit. People should not promise something and then go back on their word. It's not right. But I was not angry enough to kill the man, as you're obviously implying. I'd never even met him in person!"

Had she convinced him? She felt a little desperate, and hoped her voice didn't convey it.

"Well, then," Grant said, sweeping his gaze across the room full of people, "who did?"

At that very moment, the power went out.

The sudden cessation of the orange lamplight elicited an audible gasp from nearly every person in the room. They were still partly visible in the firelight, at least those closest to the fireplace.

The hair on Charity's neck prickled, as though a chill breeze had blown through. Was Hugo writing down "power outage" and a note of the time for the police? Details like that could be important.

After a moment of silence, Ashley stirred from her place beside the fire. "It's just the storm, I'm sure. Desmond, help me light candles."

The couple each retrieved a lighter from near the fireplace, and circled the room in opposite directions, lighting candles scattered through the room.

One by one, the party goers came to light, as candles were lit near them. Each one looked as uncomfortable as the last. The candle nearest her smelled of pine, like a winter forest.

"Where's Rowan?" Charity asked when all the

candles had been lit and the hosts had returned to their previous spots.

They each surveyed the room, but Rowan was gone.

Vera sucked in a breath. "This is always where the second body shows up."

"Too many murder mysteries, Vera." Felicia's playful tone seemed more mocking than friendly. "You should find another genre."

Charity shook her head. The comment seemed unfair. But in the candlelight, Felicia probably didn't sense her disapproval.

Let it go, Charity.

"Someone should look for Rowan." Desmond's voice was concerned. "Make sure he's OK."

A shadow appeared in the entrance to the room, in the hallway they'd all traveled, what seemed like hours ago, in response to Vera's scream outside.

And it was Vera again who let out a little shriek, though not as loud as the last.

~ *Felicia* ~

Felicia held her amusement in check at Vera's muffled gasp. It was only Rowan in the darkened doorway, back from wherever he had been.

The man seemed to sense all eyes on him, even in the half-light.

"Just using the facilities, people. Not a big deal. Although a power outage in someone else's bathroom isn't the greatest experience."

Grant was wandering through the room now, examining each person in turn, as though he would detect guilt on someone's face if he got close enough.

Hugo picked up a poker and prodded the fire beside Felicia, but from his sideways glances, it seemed like an excuse to study *her*.

Felicia avoided Hugo's eyes. In the same way she knew they were alike, she knew he could read something in her she didn't want seen.

She hadn't expected Ashley to toss the fact that she'd been interested in Vincent out to the room. It was a long time ago, and she would have thought Ashley had forgotten by now. Sure, Ashley was trying to make the point that she was no more a killer than Felicia, but Felicia's past feelings wouldn't be dismissed so easily.

Not by Grant.

She would have expected someone to suspect her, but not for that reason.

"What are you hiding, Felicia?"

She looked up at Vera, surprised. "What do you mean?"

Vera shrugged. "You seem evasive, that's all."

"So now I'm a suspect?"

Grant clapped her on the shoulder. "Yeah, I think I'm putting my money on Felicia. From what little I know of all of you, she's the only one with the *chutzpah* to do it." He narrowed his eyes at Felicia. "Always looking for the next exciting thing, right?"

It was true, she'd tried a few too many experiences in her life, looking for "the right thing," whatever that was. And maybe she struggled to avoid the whole "shiny new object" syndrome that left her avoiding commitment to anything out of a fear of missing the next best opportunity. But a love of spontaneity didn't make someone a killer, no matter what accusations Grant might toss out.

It was Rowan who came to her defense. "Nah, Felicia's way too *hakuna matata* for murder. No worries, right, girl?"

She smiled at him. Black sheep had to stick together.

"All the same," Grant said, "seems like we add you to Hugo's list of people with a possible motive."

"That's quite a list you're compiling, there, Professor." Rowan pulled himself off the couch and sauntered over near the candlelit bar, squinting at the notepad Hugo had left behind.

Hugo crossed from the fire, poker still in hand like a fencing blade, and retrieved his notepad.

"Interesting, though," Rowan continued, "how you've managed to steer everyone's attention toward anyone but yourself. Makes me wonder if you've got something to hide."

"Me?" Hugo drew himself upright. "I didn't even know the man."

Felicia had circled to the fireplace, and now cleared her throat. "Uh, I didn't want to say anything…"

"Well, you have to say it now." Charity sounded impatient. Eager to condemn or defend someone else, perhaps.

"Well, when I was checking Vincent's — body — before I realized it was him, I was looking for ID."

Grant stepped closer to her. "And?"

"And I found this in his pocket." She reached for the crinkled paper she'd hidden behind a jade green vase on the mantel. "I didn't want to mention it. I was planning to give it to the police, but I probably should have left it on him."

"What is it?" Ashley asked the question, a tightness

in her voice, as though she feared the answer.

"It's seems to be the beginning of a rough draft of some kind of article. Something Vincent was writing, I guess."

Desmond sighed. "What about it, Felicia? Spill it, if you think it's important."

She shrugged. "Seems like he was writing something up for a journal, maybe, about how the improvements that Hugo has made to Ashley's original formula for the art restoration solvent would actually be harmful to the art over time…"

"Hugo's a chemist—he would certainly know how to poison someone!" Vera tossed the accusation into the room like a bomb.

"So would Ashley." Grant this time, argumentative as always.

Hugo said nothing, only held out his hand for the paper in Felicia's hand.

She let him take it, watched him scan it.

"This is not right!" Charity ran a hand through her hair. "If that paper incriminates Hugo, you certainly shouldn't be giving it to him. You shouldn't even have taken it from the body!"

Felicia rolled her eyes, but snatched the scrap of paper from Hugo's hand and delivered it to Charity. "If you're so concerned about procedure, put it back yourself. It was in his right coat pocket."

Charity's eyes widened and she hesitated, but then stood. "Fine. If you won't do it, I will."

She disappeared down the hallway.

Felicia had to give her credit. She had the guts to stick to what she believed.

"Hugo, did you know about the article?" Ashley's voice was low, but in the heavy quiet, it might as well have been a shouted accusation.

"I knew nothing of this man."

Rowan wrapped an arm around Hugo.

"Don't worry, old man, if anyone had a big enough grudge against old Vincent to kill him, it was me."

In the shocked silence that followed this unexpected revelation, Charity burst back into the Great Room.

"He's gone!"

The other eight, still taking in Rowan's statement, were slow to turn to Charity.

"I'm telling you, someone took Vincent's body. There's nothing there!"

Rowan had to admit, he disliked being upstaged. He'd timed his confession perfectly, but then Charity had to ruin it by charging in with her big announcement about a missing body. He tapped impatient fingers against his thigh, but let Charity's announcement play out.

Ashley grabbed Charity's arm. "What do you mean?" Even in the flickering candlelight, Rowan thought Ashley's face looked like she'd aged during her birthday party.

Charity yanked her arm from Ashley's grip. "Exactly what I said! I went out to return this," she waved the paper Felicia had found in Vincent's pocket, "but he was not there!"

As if on cue, a door slammed somewhere in the house.

Vera yelped. Again.

Man, Rowan was loving this. The whole thing was deliciously spooky. A murder, the storm, the power outage. Flickering candles and slamming doors. And now a disappearing body?

But it was time to deliver his motive.

"Maybe he got dragged off by a wild animal or something. It would serve him right." Okay, that was a little harsh, but he needed some drama to bring the story back around.

"Rowan!" Ashley's face contorted into something that looked like horror. It was hard to tell.

He shrugged. "I told you, I'm the one with the biggest reason to kill that guy."

Desmond was shaking his head. "College was a long time ago, Rowan—"

"I'm talking about last month, brother. Last month. Because right around the time Vincent was pulling his donation out of CleanCity I believe, he was also giving *me* the shaft."

He had everyone's attention now, had them eating out of his hand, in fact, like any good storyteller.

"Vincent had promised me an art show in his gallery."

Ashley gasped. "Rowan, that's amazing!"

"Yeah, well, it would have been. If he hadn't yanked the rug out two weeks later." He frowned. "I was finally going to get my big break. Then... it all went away."

Desmond circled the leather sofa and threw an arm around his brother. "That's tough luck, Rowan, I'm sorry. Did he say why?"

"Nah. Nothing that made any sense to me, anyway. But I'll tell you what, I was spitting mad. Still am." He shrugged. "Though I guess it's pointless to be mad at a dead guy."

"But — but you didn't kill him, did you Rowan?" Ashley was shaking her head, as if to coach him on his answer.

He frowned at his sister-in-law. "Don't believe I have it in me?"

She opened her mouth as if to speak, then closed it again, that pained look back on her face.

It was a stupid thing to say, but he felt an unaccountable annoyance that probably no one thought him capable of murder. They'd never really understood him. His family saw him as uniquely talented, sure. But they didn't seem to realize that it could be a burden, the inability to simply get a job working for "the man" like everyone else, something he knew would kill his creative soul. He wasn't trying to avoid responsibility. He just couldn't live that workaday life like most people. But he didn't like being dismissed.

Grant pushed his way past those standing around him to face Rowan. "Speak plainly, man. Did you kill Vincent or not?"

"How about you, Mr. CEO? Since you're the one getting in everybody's face. Did you kill him?"

"Me?" Grant looked around at the others. "I didn't know him either!"

Charity turned on him. "Well then, what makes you think it's right to accuse people, when you know nothing about any of it?"

"So you're claiming you didn't know him?" Rowan had saved the best for last. "Because I know you, even if you don't know me. I've seen you around the art world. Attending shows. Buying expensive pieces. And now you're here, trying to sell Ashley your company. Maybe you got yourself into some financial trouble with your art-collecting hobby? You wouldn't be the first."

Grant huffed. "You know nothing about me!" He glanced around at everyone's stares. "Yes, I collect art. And perhaps I ran into Vincent at a show or two. Or at his gallery. But that doesn't mean—"

"Strange," Hugo interrupted, twirling his fire poker, "that like Charity, you hadn't mentioned knowing the victim, either."

Grant sputtered, obviously indignant. "I didn't know him!"

"No. Obviously not."

"If you're going to be so ridiculous as to accuse me, we might as well go back to suspecting Lily! Or Vera, for that matter!"

At this, Lily smiled placidly as though Grant had complimented her, and Vera ran a nervous hand through her already-messy hair.

Rowan was losing his moment. "I thought Vincent saw something special in my work. I still think maybe he did. I don't know what happened." He glanced at Desmond. "I'm sorry, man. I was hoping this was the year I'd make something of myself."

Desmond waved a hand, as if Rowan's emotion was of no consequence.

And perhaps the feeling of revenge was not as sweet as Rowan would have expected.

~ *Grant* ~

Grant was getting tired of the whole thing. He'd tried to take charge of the questioning, but only because that's the kind of guy he was — one who takes initiative to make things happen, and then makes decisions fast. That was how you kept people from controlling you, the way you stayed strong in the face of challenges. But it was getting old now, and Rowan was trying to turn the whole thing on him. His attempt to do it right had ended up offending people. That happened often, and he really didn't get it.

Because tonight, tonight something needed to be done.

"Let's be clear, here." He grabbed the poker from Hugo and thrust it back into the stand with a clang, pulling the attention from Rowan's sob story to himself.

"Of every person here, it sounds like I had zero motive to kill this guy. I didn't know him, and he'd never hurt anyone I cared about. Instead of accusing me," at this he glared at Rowan, "it just makes more sense for me to be the one asking questions."

"We only have your word that you didn't know him." Felicia smiled sweetly. "Why are you so intent on making us believe it?"

"Because it's the truth!"

She shrugged and glanced at her fellow guests. "If you say so."

"You think you're the one who should ask the questions, Grant?" Ashley pulled away from her spot by the gray stone wall to stare him down. "Maybe we *all* want to ask the questions!"

He threw his hands toward the beamed ceiling. "Then go ahead! What's stopping you? What's stopping any of you?"

"Fine." Ashley turned on her husband. "I want to know how you could suspect me of cheating on you? And with *him*?"

Desmond's face darkened. "I don't know, Ash, maybe because he's rich and successful, and everything you care about, everything that I'm not!"

Ashley took a step back as though she'd been slapped.

He moved toward her. "My question is why you'd reach out to him after all these years? What were you hoping to gain?" When she didn't answer, Desmond turned away. "No. Actually, my question is for Vera. Why would you tell me about those emails, when you knew how they looked, that they'd make me suspicious of my wife?"

Vera dropped her gaze to the parquet floor. "Okay, so I'm always doing the wrong thing. But I thought I was helping." She lifted her head to stare at Charity. "Now that he's dead, I'm remembering all those angry subject lines in *your* emails."

"Is that a question?"

Vera shrugged and said nothing.

Grant liked this much better. All this arguing deflected attention away from him. And the financial troubles Rowan had somehow rightly guessed.

"So we're all getting a question, now?" Charity seemed close to tears for some reason. "I want to know just how involved Felicia was with Vincent, back in college."

Felicia shrugged at Charity. "I thought he was interesting. That was all. He was into Ashley. And that was fine."

"Good. Because you wouldn't betray your sister, right?"

"I think that's two questions. I thought you liked to play by the rules."

"When was Vincent going to make his entrance?" Hugo's question was for Desmond.

Desmond sighed, as though exhausted. "Felicia was going to give him a sign when I brought out the cake." But then, annoyingly, he pointed at Grant. "Listen, you're the only one we don't really know here. I would vouch for any of these people!" He waved an arm around the group, but dropped it when it included Charity. "Well, maybe not Charity. I don't really know her either. But good grief, she runs a non-profit!"

"Ha!" Rowan clapped his hands. "There it is, folks. An airtight alibi. Do-gooders can't be do-badders!"

"May I ask my question?" Lily's voice was gentle. "Why is no one asking what happened to Vincent's body?"

The rush of hostility seemed to slam against a wall, and the room fell silent.

So silent that they all heard the *creak-creak* of the floorboards above their heads.

~ *Lily* ~

"Maybe we all should calm down." Lily had heard the creaking floors above, just like everyone else, but she chose to ignore it.

Ashley had grabbed Desmond's arm. "Maybe you should check it out."

"Nobody's going anywhere." Grant extended an arm like he'd physically stop them.

Lily glanced over toward the bar, to see if Hugo was still taking notes.

But Hugo wasn't there.

She scanned the room quickly, but didn't see him. Perhaps he was in the shadows again. He seemed to enjoy pulling away from the group whenever Grant wasn't asking questions.

Too many questions. The man seemed unable to stop.

Vera cleared her throat. "I know what my question is now. I want to know how far Lily would go, if she thought Vincent was back in Ashley's life."

Lily smiled. "Is that a question *for* me, Vera? Or simply a statement *about* me?"

Vera's head lifted, and her stare had an uncharacteristic hardness about it. "It's a question for you."

Lily hated all of this, but she also hated having any dishonesty between people. She sighed, contemplating whether the truth would bring disaster or resolution, and deciding to carefully put it out there.

"Vera, is it possible you had a reason to tell Desmond about Vincent's emails?"

The hardness remained in Vera's eyes, but her face paled a notch. "What are you talking about?"

"Maybe because you're in love with him."

"What?" She gripped the arms of her chair. "Who?"

Now that it was out there, Lily did feel sorry for the woman. "Desmond. Maybe you wanted to come between them."

Grant jumped in. "Maybe this whole thing was an elaborate way to frame Ashley for murder, so you could have Desmond to yourself!"

"No! That's not true! Like Felicia said, I would do *anything* to protect Ashley. Just like Lily!" As soon as the words were spoken, Vera bit her lip, clearly concerned that it sounded like a confession.

Lily nodded. "Okay."

"Okay?" Vera stood, trembling. "You throw out an accusation like that, and then just back down and say 'okay'"?

"I'm trying to see all the angles here, that's all. If we can get to an answer, this whole disastrous night can be over."

And truly, that was all she wanted. The conflict made her feel sick, made her wish she could run out into the snow to get away. None of their relationships would be the same after this night, and that made her sad.

"So then, what's your opinion, Lily?" Ashley slipped next to her, obviously looking for some support. "Who do you think killed Vincent?"

Lily gave Ashley a little hug. "I think I've caused enough trouble with my questions."

"So, has everyone asked enough questions, then?" Grant was back at his place against the bar. "Everyone satisfied?"

Lily sighed. "How can we be satisfied without any answers?"

Felicia huffed a little laugh. "Sounds like something Hugo would say."

Grant lifted his eyebrows. "And where is Hugo?"

That particular question hung in the room while everyone glanced around from their scattered positions.

It was official, then. Hugo had disappeared.

ACT IV

~ In Which the Culprit is Revealed ~

~ *Hugo* ~

Hugo checked his watch. Had it really only been a few hours since he'd driven up the long driveway to the estate? It seemed more like days. Though he had to admit, if only to himself, the entire thing had been much more enjoyable than he'd imagined.

He ran his fingers against the cold glass of the window set into the back door. He'd already flicked on the light, so it was easy to see where Vincent's body had lain. The poker table-top still jutted out from the mounding snow, where Vera had dropped it.

The rest of the evidence was there as well. But that would soon be taken care of.

"Hugo?"

He turned an ear toward the hall. It was Ashley's voice calling him from the Great Room. And then another, Desmond perhaps, also calling. He felt a surge of gratification. They hadn't gone calling when Rowan disappeared. Perhaps he was more connected to these people than he believed. More than just a researcher to them. That would be nice. They did invite him to this party, after all. Not that he enjoyed parties. But again, this one hadn't been all bad.

They were all clamoring for him now. His brief respite in the kitchen, away from the chaos, had clearly ended. He had needed to be alone, though. Not having answers stirred something in him, an itch he had to scratch. And sometimes, the answers could only be found when you were alone with your thoughts.

"I'm here. Coming." He traced his fingers along the wall of the dark hall as he headed back toward glow of the firelight and the smell of pine candles.

Ashley met him at the entrance, gave him an unexpected hug.

He couldn't help but smile.

"I thought something had happened to you."

"Just needed a few minutes alone. To think." He surveyed the crowd. "It's been a puzzle of a night, hasn't it? Thankfully, I believe I've solved it."

He heard, rather than saw, the inhalation of everyone in the dimly lit room.

"You know who — you know what happened to Vincent?" Ashley was still clinging to him.

He patted her hand on his arm and pulled away. "I do."

Grant folded his arms over his bulky chest. "Then tell us, Professor, and be done with it."

Hugo nearly laughed at the "Professor" moniker coming from Grant, whom Hugo had never met before tonight. He did like the nickname, though he sometimes wondered if it was prefixed with "absent-minded" when he wasn't present.

"Yes, Hugo, please." Ashley squeezed his arm. "You've been taking notes all night. Tell us what you think."

He crossed the room to stand behind the central seating area, opposite the fireplace, knowing the fire would throw light on his face.

The others shifted as well, until they ranged around him in a half-circle, with the fire at their backs, waiting.

"I will tell you what I believed happened here tonight, but you must follow my train of thought, to see how I arrived at the truth."

It was strange, to have all the attention on him after he'd stayed in the background all evening. Strange, but comfortable, now that he felt confident in his explanation.

"Let's start with Ashley. The guest of honor."

Ashley's lips parted and she glanced at Desmond.

"Ashley is a driven, success-oriented woman who needs others to think highly of her. Are these qualities enough to drive her to kill a man who once treated her badly, perhaps to keep this truth from the world?" He let the question linger, as each of them looked to Ashley. "Perhaps. But she did not kill Vincent."

Ashley's shoulders relaxed and she gave him a little smile.

"And then there is a Desmond, her long-suffering

husband. He puts up with her workaholism, because he's a good man, it seems, and he loves her. In fact, it would seem he cares about everyone he encounters. Hard to imagine that he could be driven to kill. But jealousy can be a powerful motive in even the kindest heart."

Desmond was swallowing hard, shaking his head.

"But Desmond did not kill Vincent, either." He smiled at his host, and continued.

"So we move on to the rest of the family. And we have Felicia. The impetuous and fun-loving Felicia, who loves her sister dearly, and seems just the sort of person to kill a man in a fit of… anger? Jealousy? I would think we could choose a number of reasons, couldn't we?"

Felicia had been watching him intently as he spoke, and now the side of her mouth quirked up into a half-smile.

"But you did not kill Vincent, did you, my dear?"

She shook her head, still with that half-smile.

"So we move to brother Rowan. The temperamental artist who always worries he is missing out on something. Angry at Vincent's change of plans for his art show, depressed over his lack of creative success. Emotional enough to commit murder?"

"Definitely." Rowan grinned.

"Perhaps. But Rowan did not kill Vincent."

Rowan shrugged, looking as if he were sorry to have

been acquitted.

"And now the friends and acquaintances. We start with Vera."

The woman's face twitched but she held her ground.

"The steadfast assistant, committed and responsible, though often imagining the worst. I find the suggestion that she would kill to frame her employer for murder to be ridiculous. But did she fear Ashley was in danger? Would she kill to protect her? Again, perhaps. But she did not do so tonight."

Vera's sigh of relief was audible to everyone.

"And there is Lily. Agreeable, supportive Lily, who would seem to lack the capacity for anything as heinous as murder. But as we have all said, murder may be in anyone's blood if sufficiently provoked."

Rowan raised a hand. "And don't forget, she's the least likely, so therefore the most likely."

"Yes, in the absence of a butler, I suppose we all half-expected to hear that 'the florist did it.'" Hugo smiled. "However, she did not."

The list of suspects was growing shorter, and Grant and Charity were clearly getting edgy. Grant had moved to the side of the room, hands fisted at his sides. Charity was standing firm, chin raised.

"Charity." Hugo turned to her. "We have just met,

but already I can see you are a woman of principled ideals whose greatest desire is to maintain integrity and order. I admire that, and can hardly imagine murder in your heart."

Charity's chin lowered a bit, and her eyes softened.

"However, such high ideals often mask serious rage at a world that is not what it should be, and when that rage is provoked, by someone such as Vincent, perhaps… murder."

"I could never—"

Hugo raised a hand. "No fear. You did not kill Vincent, either."

All eyes moved toward Grant.

He took a step toward Hugo, one fist slightly raised.

Hugo took a deep breath. "Grant, again we have just met, but your confident — and dare I say confrontational — manner certainly makes you seem capable of violence. However, I've also observed a strong bent toward fighting for the *right* thing in you, which makes you less likely. And no one seems able to prove that you even knew our victim. No, you did not kill Vincent, either."

The room was silent, each of them eyeing the other.

Ashley spoke first. "But, that's everyone, Hugo. Everyone, except for… you."

Hugo smiled briefly and dipped his head. "Indeed. I left myself for last. Because it was my own motive for killing Vincent that finally led me to the truth."

The room fell utterly silent.

"Charity, do you still have the paper found on Vincent — the article he was writing about my work?"

She pulled it from her pocket and fluttered it, but clearly was not going to give it up.

"I knew it!" Rowan slapped his hand against the stone fireplace. "I knew you were too quiet, sneaking around in the shadows. You did it, didn't you?"

Hugo continued as though there had been no interruption. "This was the clue that led to the solution. Our culprit overplayed things a bit here, I'm afraid. For there was no way that this supposed article was real." He extended a palm toward Charity. "If you'd be so kind as to read the title."

Charity unfolded the paper and held it up to the firelight. "*United Chemical Researcher's Newest Product is a Hazard to the Art World.*"

"Yes, and then the article itself…"

"It just talks about how you're developing some kind of microemulsion technique—"

"Microemulsion?" Ashley leaned over Charity's shoulder to look at the paper. "But that's not even Hugo's project."

"Exactly." Hugo nodded. "Someone had gotten their facts wrong. I began to suspect that the article itself was a fake. That no art gallery dealer would even be tasked with writing such a thing."

The confusion in the room was evident.

"And then we add the missing body, and it all becomes obvious."

"Uh, how about making it obvious to the rest of us, Professor." Grant smirked.

Hugo sighed. "Very well. You see, the first question I put to myself when this puzzle began was, *how could someone have slipped out to kill a guest who was meant to be a surprise?*" He waited for that idea to sink in. "The second question was, *how does a dead body disappear?*"

No one spoke. Was he the only smart person in the room?

"The answer to the first question… only someone who knew about the surprise. And the answer to the second question… when the dead man is not dead."

Still, the confusion.

Time to summarize, then.

"None of you — none of *us* — killed Vincent. He was invited here as a surprise for Ashley, albeit a somewhat uncharitable surprise, but one other person knew that Vincent was coming." He turned to the woman in the doorway of the back hall. "Felicia."

He couldn't help raising his voice a bit, for effect. "Felicia, who was the one who told us all that Vincent was dead, since of course she is the only one with medical training. And Felicia, who knew that Vincent was coming because Desmond enlisted her to give him the signal to enter via the back door."

"I - I don't understand." Ashley's voice was a whisper. "You're saying now that Felicia *did* kill him?"

"I am saying that no one killed him." He crossed the room to take Ashley's hands. "I am saying that your sister has given you the strangest birthday present I have ever seen. A fake murder!"

At that dramatic pronouncement, Felicia began to laugh.

"You did it! I knew you would!" She leaned backward into the darkened hall. "You can join us now."

And there he was, holding his coat, grinning lips still a bit artificially blue, standing in the hall.

Vincent.

~ *Finale* ~

The storm passed, unloading more snow than the county had seen in years, but it was gone by morning, replaced with a blinding sunrise and blue skies.

Desmond had finally produced the cake last night, and as they sat in the Great Room with plates of cake and coffee, Felicia confessed to the entire farce, which had gone much better than she even imagined it might, with motives and personalities popping up unexpectedly to muddy the waters. When she heard that Vincent was coming, she had looked him up and arranged the whole thing with him, just for fun. He'd thrown in a few slammed doors and creaking floorboards for some fun of his own. In the end, Felicia said, she knew that Hugo would solve it.

Aside, to only Hugo, she whispered that the murder-mystery had been as much a gift for him as for Ashley. It was the only way she could think of to get him to enjoy the party. Hugo was much surprised at the trouble she'd taken, and thought perhaps she was right — that they did have more in common than he would have thought. And there was something about that joyful spontaneity of hers that was very… interesting.

Vincent proved to be as obnoxious as ever, but by

the end of the night had committed himself to a small donation to Charity's CleanCity project and a small art show for Rowan. "Hey, if it'll keep me from getting murdered," he said. Everyone laughed, but the laughter was admittedly a bit tense.

Ashley and Desmond sat side-by-side on the couch, arms and legs touching. The appearance of the living, yet insufferable, Vincent had allayed Desmond's jealous fear, especially after Ashley explained she'd only reached out to Vincent to connect him with Charity.

Even Vera and Lily found some common ground in their affection for Ashley, and called a truce over their plates of cake.

Grant sat apart, wondering how he'd ended up in this freak show, hoping that when it was over, the possible merger with United Chemical would still be on the table.

After cake, the party guests drifted off to various guest rooms, emerging in the morning to the welcome news that the roads were now open.

And the news that the police were at the door.

By consensus, and as retribution for what she had put them all through, the group pushed Felicia into the front hall, to explain the "misunderstanding" about the dead body.

Not surprisingly, she had the two officers laughing in a matter of minutes.

And so, the party ended and the guests departed.

Each of them capable of great good, or possibly evil, in the world.

Each of them with strengths and flaws, with beauty and struggle.

Perhaps understanding themselves a bit more in the sunlight of a bright new day.

For in the end, each of us are different facets of a single, beautiful, mysterious work of art.

~ THE END ~

A Quick Note...

Hey, this is Desmond! I hope you enjoyed celebrating Ashley's birthday with us, despite... well, you know. I tried to make it a great night for Ashley, but you can't always control these things.

The author has more for you after this quick message from me. You'll learn more about the Enneagram and what "type" each of my friends and family are, plus see further resources.

But first... I'm asking for a favor. I'd love it if you'd leave a review on Amazon. The author is trying to get her work out into the world, and I'm trying to help. Reviews go far in spreading the word.

So if you enjoyed *Dressed to the Nines* could you take a minute or two and just post a few words about the story and how you felt about it?

It would be so appreciated!

Thank you!
~Desmond

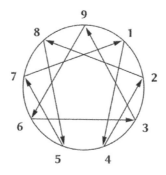

What is it and where did it come from?

First, the name... In Greek, "ennea" means *nine* and "gram" means *drawing* or *something written*. So the Enneagram is a simple name for a drawing with nine segments.

It has absolutely nothing to do with satanic rituals or the pentagram (a five-segmented drawing), in the same way that a hexagram (six-segmented) Star of David is not related to the pentagram symbol.

The Enneagram is personality-type model, and is currently experiencing a surge in popularity, but as a system of understanding the human condition, it is far from new. Its roots trace back through Greek philosophy, and through both Jewish and Christian religious thought.

How does it work?

In the Enneagram model, you usually have one primary type, or number, which represents the core of who you are, the motivations for what you do. You will usually see yourself in the description of one number, more than any other.

You will also likely have one or two "wings" which are the adjacent numbers. In other words, if you are a Four, you may have many characteristics of either a Three or a Five (or even both). This adjacent number is called your Wing. You may see people talking about their Enneagram like this: "I'm a 5w4." That means that the person is a type Five, with a Four wing.

The Enneagram model also has "arrows." Each number has an arrow moving away from it toward another number, and an arrow moving toward it. The arrow moving away represents stress, lack of health, insecurity, etc., and shows you the number whose unhealthy characteristics you tend to take on when you are in that unhealthy state. For example, our 5w4 above has an arrow moving away toward the Seven. This means that the type Five tends to take on the characteristics of a Seven, but in an unhealthy way, when he or she is not in a good place.

Likewise, there is an arrow moving *toward* each number, and this arrow represents the number whose best characteristics are taken on when that number is functioning in a secure, healthy place of growth. In our example, the type Five has an arrow moving toward it from type Eight, so the best of type Eight will show up in a healthy Five.

So who cares?

As you can see from this explanation, every person will have four or five different numbers where they see aspects of themselves: their primary Enneagram type number, one or two wings, and the numbers for stress and for growth.

Doesn't it make the system somewhat meaningless if you are claiming five out of nine numbers?

Not at all. Understanding your primary number, and the beautiful facets of your wing that you incorporate, and seeing the places in your life that clearly represent growth for you, or indicate that you are unhealthy, can be truly transformative. It has been for me.

"But I don't like being boxed in."

The Enneagram model has even more depth than what is described above, so there is much more than being "boxed in" to a single number. However, you would most likely find yourself described in the Enneagram whether you were aware of it or not. In other words, you *are* a certain type of person, whether you like that fact or not, and whether you are aware of it or not. The Enneagram is not so much about limiting you as it is about becoming aware of all the beauty and struggle that already exists within you. Understanding your type gives you a tool for growth, not a definition that ties you down.

The Enneagram also does not give you an excuse to be a rotten person. Claiming you "can't help acting this way" because of your Enneagram number is no more valid than anything else in your life you might blame. Yes, you have had influences, both internal and external, that have shaped you. But transformation, growth, and change are possible.

People sometimes mention that the Enneagram seems to paint a negative picture of each type (more so than other personality-typing systems such as Myers-Briggs). I believe that including both the strengths and struggles of each type is what makes the Enneagram so powerful. Seeing yourself clearly, even the parts that need redeeming, is a critical step in personal growth.

What follows is a simple description of each Enneagram type, and the corresponding character in *Dressed to the Nines*. Read it only after you've read the story itself.

After the section of character types and their descriptions, you will find additional information and a link to further resources. I would encourage you to keep exploring!

~ Key to the Characters ~

Warning: This section contains spoilers!

Read this section only after you've finished the story, tried to find yourself in one of the characters, and are ready for more information.

When you're ready...

Explore each of the following nine character types, and see if one of them resonates with you more than an other. Remember that your Enneagram type is based on what *motivates* you, more than simply the nickname given to the type or how you appear to other people. Your real self might buried under a few layers!

The names for each type vary, depending on whose work on the Enneagram you are reading, and these variations are included with the descriptions.

After the type descriptions, you'll find a link to more resources.

~ Charity ~

Enneagram Type One
The Perfectionist / Reformer
The Need to be Perfect[1]

Charity, head of the non-profit organization CleanCity, is our Type One. She's a person who values both personal integrity and the "rightness" of everyone and everything else in the world. She struggles with anger when things aren't done the right way. This perfectionism is often not for her own sake but for the sake of, or in defense of, other people. She doesn't like to see people harmed by the evil or corrupt forces in the world, and wants to work to eradicate injustice. She's strict and critical of herself as well, so she's at her best when she loosens up a bit, and finds joy in the good work she does.

[1] The "needs" are taken from the excellent book, *The Enneagram: A Christian Perspective*, by Richard Rohr and Andreas Ebert, Crossroad Publishing, 2001.

~ Desmond ~

Enneagram Type Two
The Helper
The Need to be Needed

Desmond, Ashley's husband, is our Type Two. He's a warm and nurturing person who seems to love everyone. A Two fears not being needed, and is often found serving others, sometimes to his own detriment. A Two struggles with a bit of pride, of admitting that he himself has needs, and would rather focus on taking care of everyone else. When he's at his best, he's taking care of both others and himself, and he is one of the most generous of all the types.

~ Ashley ~

Enneagram Type Three
The Achiever / Performer
The Need to Succeed

Ashley, a Type Three, loves meeting goals and getting things done, and she loves being seen as the go-to person for whatever needs doing. Sometimes a Three can wear a mask to make sure people don't see any cracks in her ability to "do it all." A Three's fear of being worthless and desire to feel valuable causes her to push herself harder than she should, until she crashes and checks out when it all gets to be too much. A Three is at her best when she works with others to accomplish goals.

~ Rowan ~

Enneagram Type Four
The Individualist / Creative / Romantic
The Need to be Unique

Rowan, the Type Four artist in our story, tends to be unconventional and to enjoy a bit of the dramatic. He always feels a bit on the outside, as if he's different, flawed, or just doesn't belong, and is always trying to find his identity. He's self-aware and self-conscious, and feels criticism deeply. The idea of beauty is important to the Four - expressing it, enjoying it, sustaining it. A Four is often an artist, writer, or creator of some kind.

~ Hugo ~

Enneagram Type Five
The Investigator / Observer / Specialist
The Need to Understand

    The researcher Hugo is a Type Five. He is our story's "detective" because a Five has an innate problem-solving nature and a need to gather knowledge to understand the world around him. A Five is often an introvert, preferring to focus on thoughts and ideas rather than interact socially. A Five is able to understand complex ideas and often will be found researching, and perhaps teaching, these ideas. A Five sometimes struggles to connect with people, and is at his best when he steps out confidently to share with the world.

~ Vera ~

Enneagram Type Six
The Loyalist / Skeptic
The Need to be Sure

Vera, our Type Six, is all about security and support. She isn't fond of new things, change, or situations she can't predict, but this also means that a Six is more loyal and committed to people and ideas she trusts than any other type. A Six is usually the responsible one, the person who works hard to make sure everything is just as it should be. A Six may struggle with anxiety, and is at her best when she relaxes a bit and tries not to see the worst, or the potential for it, in every situation.

~ Felicia ~

Enneagram Type Seven
The Enthusiast / Visionary
The Need to Avoid Pain

Felicia, our Type Seven, is always looking for the next great adventure. A Seven throws herself into whatever she's doing, and sometimes struggles to commit, out of fear of missing the next great thing. A Seven loves life, usually loves to be with people, and is generally "the life of the party." A Seven can struggle with feeling like life is satisfying, always wondering if there is something better, and not feeling content. A Seven loves variety and gets bored easily. She's at her best when her spontaneity is tempered with enough focus to commit to goals.

~ Grant ~

Enneagram Type Eight
The Challenger / Controller
The Need to be Against

Grant is a Type Eight. He doesn't do anything small, loves a good argument, and brings an energy you can feel into any situation. An Eight can sometimes be seen as too blunt, too assertive, but he doesn't speak his mind to hurt people, and often can't tell why they take offense. He loves taking on a challenge and has great energy for leadership. An Eight's desire to control can go a bit too far, stemming from a desire for self-protection, so he's at his best when he uses his strength to improve the life of other people, showing care for them.

~ Lily ~

Enneagram Type Nine
The Peacemaker
The Need to Avoid

Lily is our Type Nine. A Nine is at the "top" of the Enneagram circle, and can usually see all the other viewpoints quite well, making her uniquely gifted at bringing people tighter and creating harmony. A Nine has a strong desire to create that harmony, in fact, and a fear of people being in conflict with each other. A Nine can struggle with voicing her own opinion and often goes with the flow to avoid conflict, so she's at her best when she puts some energy toward her own life, and being her own person.

~ *Further Resources* ~

There is more to explore!

We haven't even discussed the way in which the nine Enneagram types divide into three *triads*, or *centers* — in which you primarily act from the head, the heart, or the gut, or put another way, with thinking, feeling, or action. There are also sub-types that explore the ways we each are driven to express our individual type.

My own journey with the Enneagram began a few years ago, in reading the book *The Enneagram: A Christian Perspective* by Richard Rohr and Andreas Ebert, and then further guided by *The Road Back to You* by Ian Cron. This story has been influenced especially by the work of Ian Cron, Richard Rohr, and Don Riso.

In the past few years the Enneagram has been an important tool for me, helping me to become aware of unhealthy patterns of thought and behavior and showing the specific ways I struggle and can grow. I truly believe that we are each created to be unique reflections of God, and that in learning more about ourselves we can better love others and serve the God who made us. In fact, I believe that it's our responsibility to understand both our unique strengths and struggles, and to allow our failings to be refined so that we can better use our gifts.

I've been especially influenced by these writers on the Enneagram, and would encourage you to check out their works and websites, listed at the web address below, to proceed further on your own Enneagram journey. This short story has only been to whet your appetite, and leave you eager to learn more!

For more information and resources, see:
tracyhigley.com/enneagram-resources

~ *About the Author* ~

Tracy started her first novel at the age of eight, and hasn't stopped writing stories since. She's the author of thirteen novels, and her love of history and travel has taken her around the world to research many of her books. When not writing, she's the CEO of several small businesses, a wife, and a mom of four. She's also the founder of Impactivity, which coaches entrepreneurial women to thrive by integrating business, health, and spirituality.

~ *Also by Tracy Higley* ~

Get links to all Tracy's books here:
https://tracyhigley.com/novelist

Made in the USA
Monee, IL
14 June 2020

33656198R00069